This **WALKER** book

belongs to:

_____

_____

For Thomas Sankara, African revolutionary, who knew that "women hold up the other half of the sky". And for my father, who was his friend. **A.**

For my father, the first African in my life – I wish he'd seen this book. **M.F.**

Note from the Author:

Africa is changing all the time: new countries are being created and old traditions are being swallowed up. This book can only give an idea of what Africa is like right now as I'm writing it. I think that all the information is correct – we have double- and triple-checked it – but everyone makes mistakes. So please forgive any that you might find, and enjoy this book for what it is: a tiny glimpse into this most amazing continent.

First published 2020 by Walker Books Ltd 87 Vauxhall Walk, London SE11 5HJ • Text © 2020 Atinuke • Illustrations © 2020 Mouni Feddag • The right of Atinuke and Mouni Feddag to be identified as author and illustrator respectively of this work has been asserted by them in accordance with the Copyright, Designs and Patents Act 1988 • This book has been typeset in Clarendon T and Gill Sans MT Schoolbook • Printed in China • All rights reserved. No part of this book may be reproduced, transmitted or stored in an information retrieval system in any form or by any means, graphic, electronic or mechanical, including photocopying, taping and recording, without prior written permission from the publisher. • British Library Cataloguing in Publication Data: a catalogue record for this book is available from the British Library • ISBN 978-1-4063-7658-6 • www.walker.co.uk • 10 9 8 7 6 5 4 3 2 1

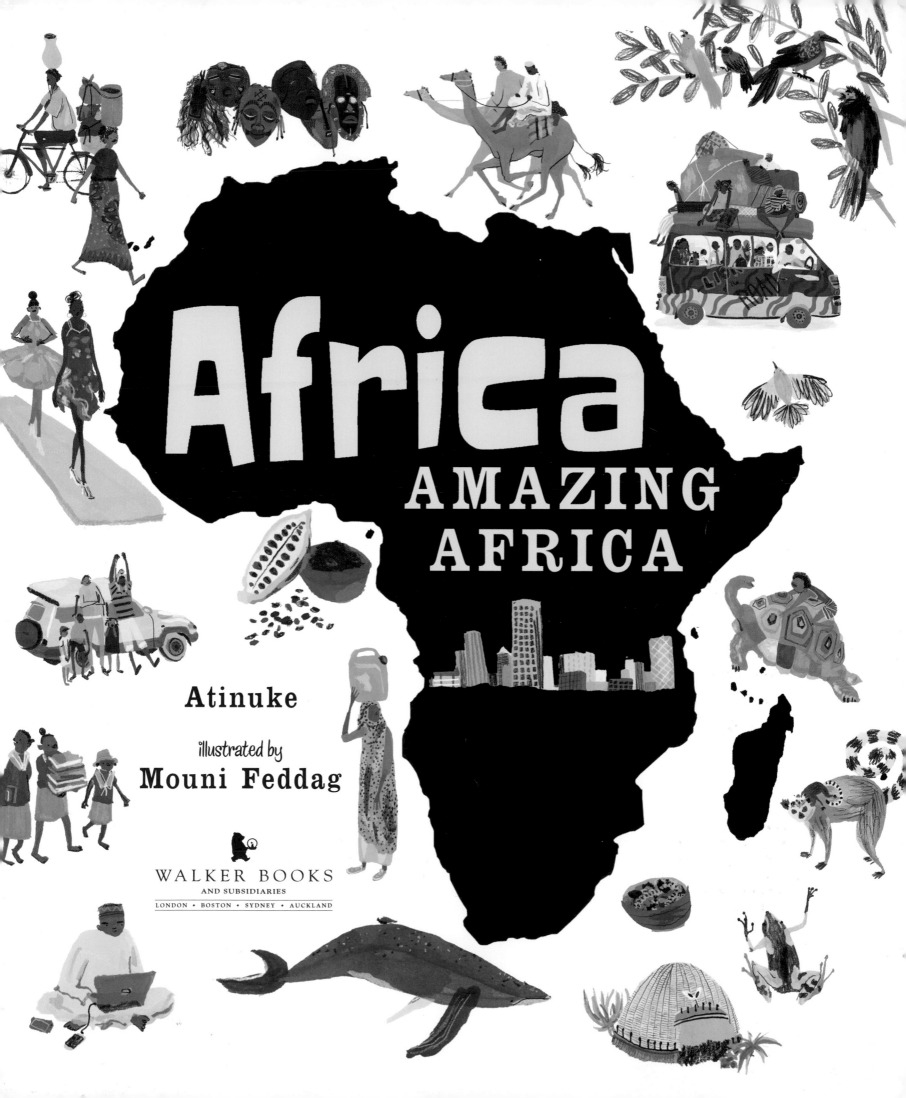

Africa
AMAZING AFRICA

Atinuke

illustrated by
Mouni Feddag

WALKER BOOKS
AND SUBSIDIARIES
LONDON · BOSTON · SYDNEY · AUCKLAND

Contents

Central Africa ... 56

North Africa ... 68

Introduction

WRITING this book has been an adventure. I wanted to write it so that I could share the things that I find exciting about Africa. But while I was working on it I found out a zillion more really exciting things.

Did you know that the first human beings to walk this earth were African? They went on to populate the whole planet. So we are all from Africa, originally!

Did you know that Africa is gigantic? It is as big as Europe, the USA, Mexico, India and Japan all put together!

Did you know that no one can decide on the official number of African countries? This is because there are countries that are still unofficial. These are new countries that are struggling to become independent from old countries.

Did you know that in each modern African country many different languages are spoken? This is because African countries are made up of lots of ancient African kingdoms. Those original kingdoms all had their own languages and customs that still exist.

Africa is not one place. It has at least 55 different countries. And each country has many different cultures, different histories, and lots of different landscapes. African countries must be the most diverse on the planet!

Africa is hot, blinding deserts; wild, wet deltas; dark, dripping rainforests; white, sandy beaches; flat, grassy savannahs; cold, snowy mountains; black volcano islands; deep blue oceans and more...

Africa is modern mega-cities with skyscrapers and motorways.

Africa is ancient cities of clay with mosques and libraries. Africa is villages of huts with goats and chickens. Africa is shanty-towns made out of cardboard and corrugated iron.

Africa is donkeys and diamonds, camels and Coca-Cola, lions and Lamborghinis, oil-rigs and armies, football and voodoo, and more...

Africa is people – more than one billion people when I was writing this book and more born every day. Almost half the people on the continent are young people – we have the youngest population on the planet!

Africa is also animals – thousands of incredible animals that are quickly becoming extinct. These animals were hunted for millennia by hunter-gathering people who never threatened their existence. It is our modern lifestyles that are wiping them out.

Climate change is changing landscapes and cultures and the lifestyles and habitats of both animals and peoples. And so is the modern technological age that is taking over the world.

Some African countries are incredibly modern, with cutting-edge hospitals and cyber-cities and fancy sports cars. Other countries are old-fashioned, with people herding camels and goats, and walking miles to collect water. Most, in fact, are both. Africa has always been a mixture of ancient traditions and innovations.

Africa had the first university in the world, more than 200 years before Europe; and centres of learning thrived there more than 1,000

years before that. It was in Africa that medicine, engineering, maths and astronomy were all developed. African scholars knew that the earth was round and circled the sun centuries before European scholars did. The first alphabets were invented in Africa, as well as the idea of counting in tens.

Today, inventors from African countries are making discoveries in medicine, robotics, software engineering, sustainable technology, banking and more.

The world has a lot to thank Africa for!

This book is a celebration of Africa. But there is a lot of heartbreak as well. There is still slavery, still war, still hunger. We are one global village now, so to make Africa a better place, we have to make the whole world a better place. That means we can start right where we are. Buying Fairtrade things, even if they are more expensive, is one way to start. If we are willing to eat less, and own less, then other people can eat more.

I could not squeeze everything that I know and love about Africa into this book. There is only room to say two or three things about each country. But hopefully this book will make you want to find out more … about the most amazing continent on the planet!

Atinuke

Southern Africa

Angola, Botswana, Lesotho, Malawi, Mozambique, Namibia, South Africa, Swaziland, Zambia and Zimbabwe

Southern Africa has long white beaches on the Indian and Atlantic Oceans, where people swim with whales and dolphins. Southern Africa has wide open savannah, where giraffes, zebras, and rhinos roam, and hunters used to stalk them. Southern Africa has the oldest deserts in the world, where, over millions of years, antelope, elephants, lions and humans have learnt to live. Southern Africa has some of the most modern cities in the world, with big banks, cutting-edge hospitals, huge museums and crazy nightclubs. Most Southern Africans have African ancestors, but some have ancestors from Europe, or India. So just like in America and Britain there are black and white and Asian Southern Africans and tons of mixed heritage people as well.

Welcome to Southern Africa!

"Mauya!" (Shona), "Ngiyanemukela!" (Zulu),

"Welkom!" (Afrikaans), "Siyalemukela!" (Ndebele)

"Namkelekile!" (Xhosa), "Welcome!" (English)

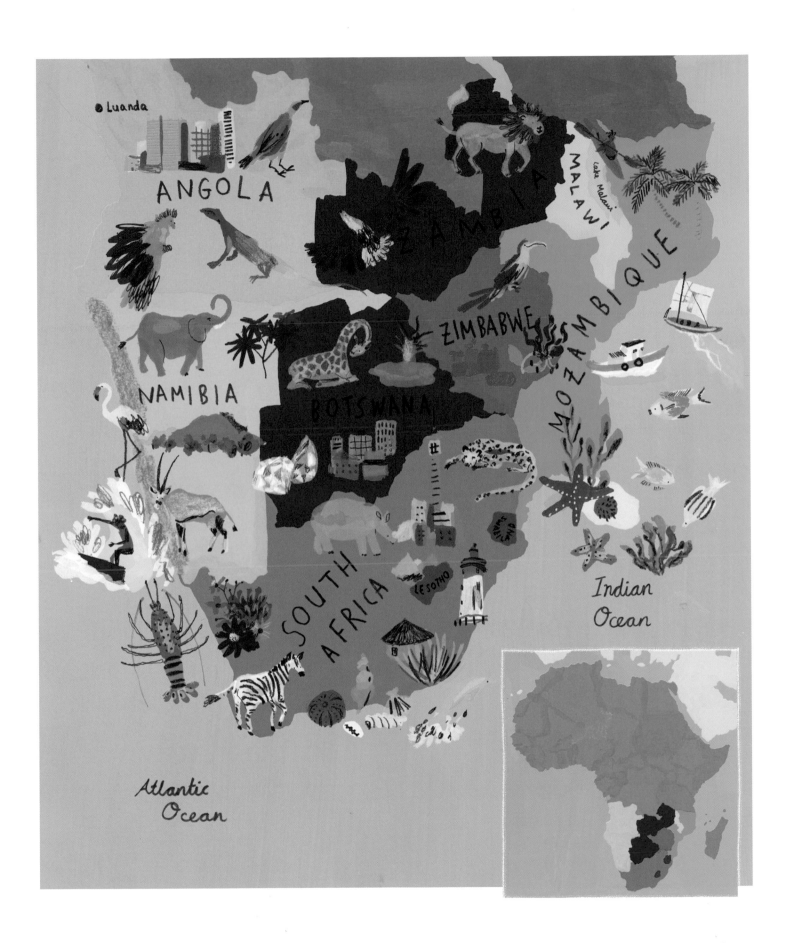

Luanda

ANGOLA

ZAMBIA

MALAWI

Lake Malawi

MOZAMBIQUE

NAMIBIA

ZIMBABWE

BOTSWANA

SOUTH AFRICA

LESOTHO

Indian Ocean

Atlantic Ocean

Angola

Angola's capital city Luanda is right on the beach where skyscrapers overlook palm trees and big white yachts in the bay. In the offices, people are busy on their computers and mobile phones; and in the streets people are busy shouting their wares and honking their car horns. Outside the city is the rainforest: a place where the forest people tread silently with their spears and arrows. A place busy with butterflies, birds, monkeys and lizards. A rainforest thick with trees that help our planet to breathe.

★ Basketball is very popular in Angola. Many of Angola's basketball players are signed by international teams.

* Angola supplies the world with oil and diamonds.

● The Brazilian martial art of Capoeira probably came from Angola.

Botswana

Botswana is rich in diamonds, rich in cattle, and rich in wildlife. It is home to millionaires, home to cattle-herders, and home to hunter-gathering people. The millionaires want to dig up the land and mine it for diamonds. The cattle-loving people want the land free of predators so their cattle can graze safely. To them, cattle are riches. The nomadic San people do not care about diamonds or cattle, they want the land to stay wild and free – just like them.

⚬ In the Tsodilo Hills of the Kalahari desert is a gallery of rock paintings and carvings by ancient nomadic peoples. They say it's on that very spot, that the creation of the world began.

✳ Black rhinos were once totally extinct in Botswana, and white rhinos were so endangered that the people of Serowe made their land into a rhino sanctuary. White rhinos multiplied there, and one day a black rhino crossed the border from Zimbabwe into the sanctuary. Now there are four black rhinos living happily in Botswana!

Lesotho

Lesotho is one of the highest countries in the world so it is called "Kingdom in the Sky". Some places can only be reached on foot or in tiny planes. It is snowy in winter and the skiing is great; but it's also very cold, so blankets are important. People don't just sleep under them – they wear them during the day. Now there are factories in Lesotho making clothes for Gap and Saks and Foot Locker, and people wear coats and jackets just as often as they wear their traditional blankets.

* There are fossilized dinosaur footprints in Lesotho, which are more than 180 million years old!

⊚ Lesotho sells electricity and water to its big neighbour South Africa. A massive dam in the highlands tunnels water to South Africa — making electricity as it goes.

Malawi

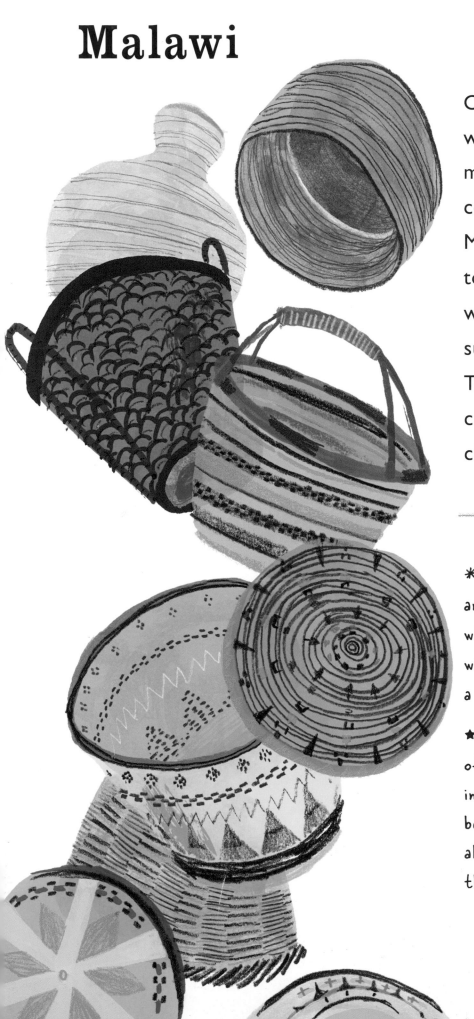

Once, Malawi was famous for its woven baskets and carved wooden masks. Now it's known for its car fuel! Petrol is expensive in Malawi, so to make cars cheaper to run Malawians experimented with mixing ethanol (made from sugarcane or corn) with petrol. Then they invented a kit that lets cars use ethanol alone. It's a very cheap way to get around.

---

* Malawi has some great young inventors and engineers. William Kamkwamba is one — when he was fourteen he built a working windmill from old scrap metal after seeing a diagram in a library book.

★ Lake Malawi has more than 1,000 sorts of fish, and most of them are found only in the lake. These fish are so bright and beautiful that they are sold to pet shops all over the world for people to put in their tropical fish tanks.

Mozambique

Football is Mozambique's favourite sport. In cities, people crowd into football stadiums to watch their favourite teams play. In towns, children who are lucky enough, practise on football pitches, and those who aren't play on the streets. In villages, children play on any bit of flat ground. And if there's not a real football, they'll make one out of rags, or plastic bags, or bark, or rubber bands, or … anything, really!

✹ Peri-peri sauce comes from Mozambique and the tiny chilli peppers that grow there are called "piri-piri" in Swahili.

◉ Mozambique's national music is called "Marrabenta". It is changing fast as it mixes with hip-hop and rap, but some things stay the same – the rhythms still make people jump up and dance!

Namibia

In Namibia, there is a desert that runs right into the Atlantic Ocean – and there you'll find some of the biggest sand dunes on the planet. These pink and orange dunes are so enormous people surf down them! The beaches are foggy because the hot desert air hits the cold Atlantic Ocean air and turns into fog. The fog stops ships seeing the jagged rocks along Namibia's coastline, so more than 1,000 shipwrecks are scattered on those foggy beaches, along with the bones of whales and seals. No wonder it's called "Skeleton Coast"!

★ In 2016 a shipwreck was discovered buried in the sand. It was a Portuguese ship that disappeared in 1533 on its way to India. On board were gold coins and ivory worth more than £9 million.

✳ There is a salt desert in Namibia, so white it can be seen from space. Another of Namibia's deserts used to sparkle not with salt but diamonds which you could collect just by running your hands through the sand!

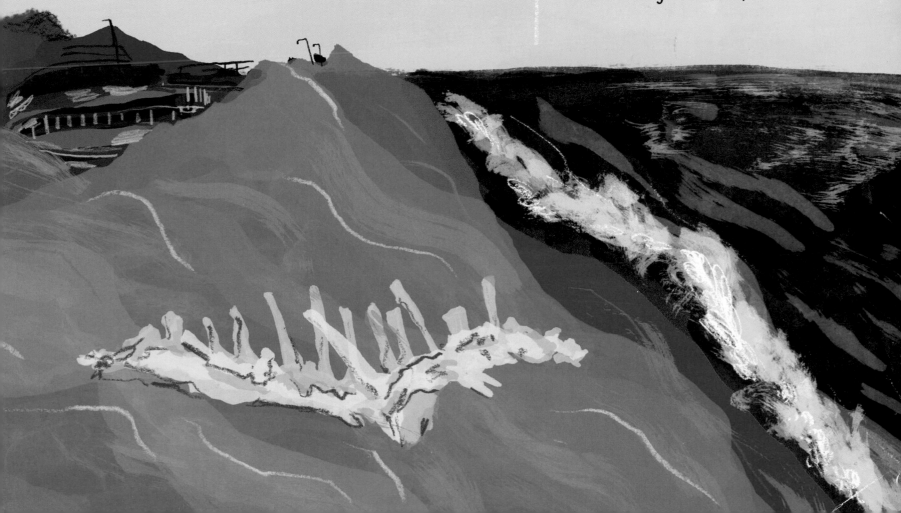

South Africa

South Africa is called the "Rainbow Nation" because of its mix of white and black and Asian people. Once there was a terrible conflict between the groups, when some of the white people decided they were better than anyone else, and kept jobs, land and education just for themselves. Other people, like Nelson Mandela, fought for everybody to be considered equal. Now the battle is over and South Africans are working together for peace. It is one of Africa's most modern countries: there are big cities like Johannesburg and Cape Town with football stadiums, shopping malls, mansions and ghettos, where all sorts of different people live and work and play.

● Nelson Mandela was the first black South African president. During the conflict he was kept in prison for 27 years. He was told he would only be freed if he stopped fighting for equality for all South Africans. He always refused!

✱ There are lots of car factories in South Africa: BMW, Chrysler, Fiat, Ford, General Motors, Mercedes Benz, Nissan, Toyota and Volkswagen. And it has its own car makes too, like Advanced Automotive Design, Bailey Cars, Birkin Cars and Perana Cars.

Swaziland

The King of Swaziland is the last proper king in all of Africa. King Mswati III has been king since he was eighteen years old and everybody has to do what he says – the parliament, the newspapers, even the army and the police. Mswati has lots of cars, lots of palaces and even lots of wives. He is very, very rich, but most of the Swazi people are very, very poor.

★ Traditional houses in Swaziland are beautiful domes made of reeds and grasses.

● When there's a festival in Swaziland people love to dress in bright traditional clothes, dance traditional dances, and sing traditional songs, all of which have not changed for hundreds of years. "The land is all for the king" is one of the songs!

Zambia

In Zambia lots of people carry things on their heads: baskets, buckets and even sacks. It's much easier to carry heavy things with our strong neck muscles than with our skinny arms. And Zambians can do this without using their hands to hold things steady – even when they are running or riding motorbikes. It's beautiful, it's skilful, it's fun – and it's done all over Africa.

⚫ On the border between Zambia and Zimbabwe is the biggest waterfall on the planet. It is called "Mosi-oa-Tunya", which means "the smoke which thunders", because when spray from the falling water hits the river below it looks like smoke and can be seen as far as 30–50 km away. In English, it is called "Victoria Falls".

★ Every year 10 million or more fruit bats gather in Zambia. It's the biggest mammal-migration on Earth!

Zimbabwe

Zimbabwe has incredible structures. It has modern cities full of skyscrapers and sculptures. It has the ancient ruined city of Great Zimbabwe. And most incredible of all it has the balancing rocks in Matobo National Park. Some of these are rocks the size of cars, balanced on rocks the size of houses, balanced on rocks the size of football stadiums. Others are massive rocks the size of lorries, balanced on rocks the size of Minis, balanced on rocks the size of shopping trolleys. These rocks have not wobbled for millions of years – so people not only climb them, they actually build houses in their shade!

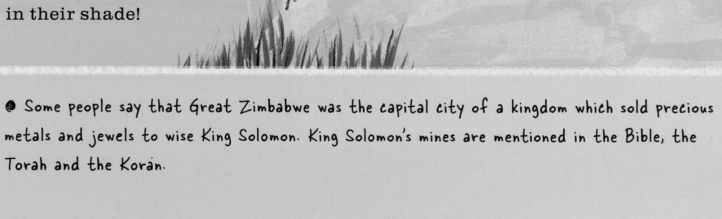

◉ Some people say that Great Zimbabwe was the capital city of a kingdom which sold precious metals and jewels to wise King Solomon. King Solomon's mines are mentioned in the Bible, the Torah and the Koran.

East Africa

Comoros, Djibouti, Eritrea, Ethiopia, Kenya, Madagascar, Mauritius, Rwanda, Seychelles, Somalia, South Sudan, Sudan, Tanzania and Uganda

East Africa is famous for its huge savannahs where Africa's most popular animals live – elephants, lions, giraffes, zebras and lots more. Out of those savannahs rise Africa's tallest mountains, and there you will find its deepest lakes, and most powerful waterfalls. East Africa is the part of Africa closest to Asia. For more than one thousand years ships have come across the Indian Ocean from Asia bringing tea, spices, silks and gunpowder to swap for East African ebony, ivory, gold, salt and labour. The Arab nations were also involved in the trade. After centuries of doing business together the East African language of Swahili has lots of Asian and Arabic words. The Swahili city states were thriving hundreds of years before Europe knew Africa (or even America) existed. Swahili is still the most important language in East Africa. And East Africa is still a melting pot of many different continents, cultures, traditions and religions.

Welcome to East Africa!

"Karibu!" (Swahili), "iNikwaNi dehiNa MeT'ahi!" (Amharic), "Baga nagaan dhufte!" (Oromo), "Soo dhowow" (Somali), "ahlan bik!" (Arabic)

Mediterranean Sea

Suez Canal

Red Sea

SUDAN

ERITREA

DJIBOUTI
Djibouti

ETHIOPIA

SOUTH SUDAN

SOMALIA

Indian Ocean

UGANDA

KENYA
Nairobi

RWANDA Lake Victoria

TANZANIA

COMOROS

SEYCHELLES

MADAGASCAR

MAURITIUS

Indian Ocean

Comoros

There are hundreds of mosques on the islands of Comoros where people go to pray. Some are big and grand, others are small and shabby. Most children go to Koranic schools where they learn to read and write in flowing Arabic script, and study the Koran, Islam's holy book. All over the island grow beautiful scented flowers. They are used to make sweet-smelling oils that are sold all over the world to make perfumes. Some of the oils are even considered holy.

✦ Comoros is a group of four islands: Grande Comore, Moheli, Anjouan and Mayotte.

"HELLO!" (Arabic)

● Islam is the biggest religion in the Comoros. Laws in Comoros are mainly drawn from Islamic religious and common law.

Djibouti

For over 3,500 years, ships from Africa and Asia and Europe have stopped in Djibouti to trade. Even today the capital city is one of the busiest ports in the world, where container ships refuel and change cargo. Outside the city, the land is mostly desert where nomads live. People say it is like the moon, with its white salt lakes and cracked earth and tall rocky pillars that puff out steam.

● The white salt lake Assal is the lowest place on the whole African continent – 155m below sea level!

★ Djibouti culture is a mixture of African, French and Arabic cultures.
Even the food is a mixture. Sambusa is the name of a popular Djiboutian snack food – they are just like Indian samosas.

Eritrea

Eritrea is home to many nomadic peoples who live in tents made of woven mats that let in cool breezes. They are constantly on the move, chasing the rains that fill the wells and water the grass that their goats, camels and cattle need to thrive. Nomads depend on their herds for meat and milk as the land is too dry to grow food. The nomadic way of life is the oldest human lifestyle on the planet. But nomads are modern now, too – some use GPS and mobile phone apps to check where the rain and the best grass is.

---

* In Eritrea's war of independence (1961-91), more than a third of the army were women.

◎ There are almost 600 species of bright and beautiful birds in Eritrea. It's on a migration route – so many of the same birds can be seen in Europe, too.

Ethiopia

Ethiopia was one of the first Christian countries in the whole world – maybe the very first! In those days, Christians were often attacked for their beliefs so many churches in Ethiopia were built in safe places in the high mountains – places that were hard to get to. Some are carved into underground rocks, and others built so high up in cliffs that you have to climb to reach them. Inside, they are painted with huge beautiful and bright murals of Christian saints, kings, apostles and angels.

● In the 1880s European countries seized all of Africa except Ethiopia. This inspired other African countries when they began their long fight for independence. And it inspired Rastafarians too. They took their name from Ethiopia's last Emperor "Ras Tafari".

✷ It is thought that coffee first came from Ethiopia – and from there, the habit of drinking it spread all over the world.

Kenya

Kenya is famous for its lions, elephants, giraffes, zebras, rhinoceroses and hippopotamuses. But its city life is as wild and wonderful as its wildlife.

In the crowded streets of the capital, Nairobi, people of African, Indian, Chinese, Arabic and European descent hustle and bustle in and out of shopping malls, jumping on and off the colourful buses, chatting into their phones – or doing their online banking!

◉ The country of Kenya is named after its tallest mountain – Mount Kiinyaa. "Kiinya" is thought to mean "God's resting place".

✿ Nairobi is right on the edge of Nairobi National Park – only a powerful electric fence stops the animals roaming the city streets. The giraffes in the park have a good view of the skyscrapers downtown. And in the city, you really can see giraffes on the horizon!

Madagascar

Madagascar is an island that broke away from Africa and into the Indian Ocean 88 million years ago. There are 200,000 species of animals there and about 80 per cent of them cannot be found anywhere else on the planet. There are chameleons as big as cats, geckos that look like dead leaves and some of the frogs are the colour of tomatoes!

* There were no people on Madagascar when the island broke away. The first people to arrive came from Indonesia and Malaysia. Even now, the food, languages and customs of Madagascar are mostly Southeast Asian.

* Humpback whales come to the coast of Madagascar to breed. It is one of the best places in the whole world for watching them jump and listening to them sing.

Mauritius

Mauritius is the only African country where Hinduism is the main religion. Around half of all Mauritians are Hindu – the others are mainly Christian or Muslim. Hinduism is an Indian religion that worships lots of different gods in beautiful golden temples. Mauritian money is called "rupee", just as it is in India. This is because most people in Mauritius are descended from Indian immigrants. The rest are from Africa, China, or Europe. And they are all immigrants, too, because nobody lived on the island at all until 1683!

● There were no predators on Mauritius until humans came. And, with nothing to be afraid of, the birds forgot how to fly and grew huge. One species was called the Dodo. Dodos are now extinct – they were too easily caught by the hungry sailors who discovered the island.

★ There is a cyber-city on the island, where techies work in high-tech facilities.

✳ Ameenah Gurib became the first woman president of Mauritius in 2015. She is not only a politician – she is also a world-famous biologist.

Rwanda

Rwanda means "land of a thousand hills". It is a tiny country high up in the mountains, which has almost no flat places. The roads go either up, up, up … or down, down, down. The hills and mountains of Rwanda are farmed to grow tea and coffee that's sold all over the world. It's hard to grow things on steep slopes, so the farmers cut little flat fields into the mountains – making them look like giant green curving steps.

✱ Some mountains are still covered with wild forests, where rare mountain gorillas thrive. Daddy gorillas are over 6 feet tall and their arms can reach over 8 feet! They know how to open poachers' traps to rescue their loved ones … and they care for motherless babies too.

Seychelles

Seychelles is a country made up of 115 islands! They're all full of beautiful birds, astonishing animals and peculiar plants – rare black parrots and giant tortoises, trees with fruit like jellyfish and the biggest nuts in the world! Luckily, Seychelles has the smallest population in Africa so there is plenty of room for the birds, animals and plants. In fact, more than half of the islands have been made into nature reserves.

● Creole is an official language in Seychelles. Creole is a language made up of other languages. It's such a mix that it's incomprehensible to speakers of the original languages.

Somalia

Somali people love poetry. Once they recited poetry as they herded their flocks on land and fished on the ocean. But war, drought and famine came. And big foreign fishing trawlers that scooped up all the fish. Now some of those herdsmen and fishermen make a living as real life pirates chasing huge container ships in their little speedboats. But Somali poets are their nation's true heroes, and they are still creating poetry.

★ Sir Mo Farah, one of the greatest athletes the world has ever known, was born in Somalia to Somali parents and lived there until he was eight. He is famous for winning double golds!

✤ Somali people live all over the world now; many are refugees from war, famine and drought.

South Sudan

South Sudan is a very traditional country where the Dinka and Nuer people grow their own food and herd fierce, long-horned cattle. Many children learn at home instead of going to school. Girls learn how to grow food, and boys learn how to look after the cattle. Boys are given a young bull of their own. The boys and their bulls grow up together and are even called by the same name – a bull name.

● South Sudan has the biggest savannah in Africa. These unfenced grasslands go on for thousands of kilometres and huge herds of wild animals live there.

* A herd of cattle is like money in the bank. The more you have the more important you feel. And if you need cash you can sell a cow – like using your cash card!

Sudan

Sudan is one of the hottest and driest countries in the world. As camels can go months without drinking they used to be the most popular mode of transport before cars were invented. There are still camel markets everywhere, and camel races that are loud and colourful and fun. Watch out though – grumpy camels spit down on people from their great height and their burps and farts can go on for two minutes! But the people in Sudan are some of the friendliest in the world.

★ There are more pyramids in Sudan than there are in Egypt. Both countries were once part of the ancient Kush kingdom, ruled from Sudan by the Nubian people. The Nubians were incredible archers and invented alphabetic writing.

✱ The Blue Nile River and the White Nile River meet in Sudan. If you stand on the bridge where they meet, you can see their two different colours flowing side by side.

Tanzania

Tanzania is a country in two parts: the mainland of Tanganyika and the island of Zanzibar. The mainland is famous for the millions of animals that travel up its enormous Serengeti savannah each year, following the rain that ripens the grass. They have to cross rivers full of hungry crocodiles lying in wait — so not all of them make it! Zanzibar is famous for its busy markets, rich in the scents of spices and the voices of merchants from all around the world.

* Thousands of years ago, sailors from Indonesia and India brought nutmeg, cloves, vanilla and cinnamon to Zanzibar. The plants grow there still.

* When Tanganyika and Zanzibar became one country, a new word was created: "Tanzania".

@ Africa's tallest mountain, snow-capped Mount Kilimanjaro, rises out of the Serengeti.

Uganda

Trucks, coaches, buses, taxis and matatu-minibuses are everywhere in Uganda. The drivers won't set off until the bus is overflowing and drop passengers off wherever they shout "stop"! Old people squash together on seats with their shopping bags, and young people hang out of windows clutching their college books and laughing into their phones. Chickens and goats are squeezed in too, and roof-racks groan under bags and packages and huge bunches of bananas.

● Lake Nyanza is the biggest tropical lake in the world: 45% of it is in Uganda, 6% is in Kenya and 49% is in Tanzania. It is the size of a small country. The first European who saw it was so amazed he called it after the most awesome person he knew – Queen Victoria!

✱ Dividing the countries of Uganda and Democratic Republic of the Congo are the beautiful, snow-capped, glacial "Mountains of the Moon" (or "Ruwenzori Mountains").

West Africa

Benin, Burkina Faso, Cabo Verde, Cote d'Ivoire, the **Gambia, Ghana, Guinea, Guinea-Bissau, Liberia, Mali, Niger, Nigeria, Senegal, Sierra Leone** and **Togo**

In the north of West Africa lies the Sahara desert. In the south are the windy beaches of the Atlantic Ocean. In between is the starry Sahel where the desert meets the grassy savannahs; the savannahs merge into dark rainforests which melt into the wet mangrove swamps. The busy crowded cities rock to the rhythms of highlife and hip-hop because, whether they are blue-eyed desert nomads or dark black city dwellers, West Africans love music. Wherever you go, men wear long flowing embroidered robes over loose baggy trousers – when they are not wearing blue jeans. Once camels carried West African gold across the Sahara to the Middle East, and some of the world's first universities were founded in the region. Now West Africa sells diamonds, and oil via container ships, and highly-educated West African doctors, lawyers, and engineers work all over the world.

Welcome to West Africa!

"E K'aBO!" (Yoruba), "Sannu!" (Hausa), "Nnoo!" (Igbo), "How far?" (Pidgin), "Kusheh-o" (Krio), "Bienvenue!" (French), "Akwaaba" (Twi), "Dalal ak diam!" (Wolof), "Woezor!" (Ewe) "Ini sogoma!" (Bambara), "Welcome!" (English)

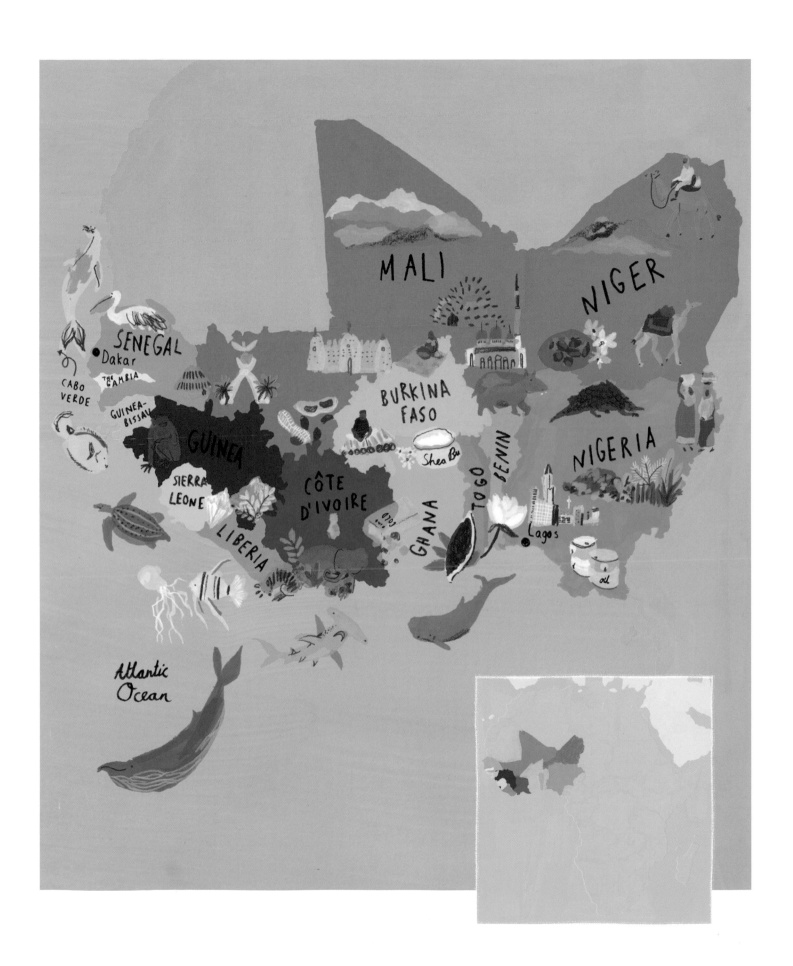

African Religions

Religion is very important in Africa. Christianity and Islam are the most popular organised religions but there are traditional religions too. They teach that everything in the world has a soul – even trees, even rocks, even rivers, even storms! It is the oldest religious belief in the world and one that all our ancestors shared. Traditional religions have many gods – some kind and some cruel – all ruled over by one top god.

Christianity and Islam arrived in Africa as soon as they were begun. Disciples who knew Jesus (in the first century) and Mohamed (in the seventh century) came to Africa to spread their religions. Some of the oldest mosques in the world are in North Africa. Some of the oldest churches in the world are in East Africa. And some of the oldest synagogues in the world are in Africa too.

Christian and Muslim soldiers tried to destroy the traditional religions – but they didn't succeed. Most Africans are now either Christian or Muslim but they still honour their traditional gods with drumming, dancing and gifts.

Benin

The traditional religion "Voodoo" is one of Benin's official religions. It is celebrated with festivals of drumming and dancing. Some people say magic is performed at these festivals too. Voodoo was taken to the Americas by Africans hundreds of years ago. And it is also one of Haiti's official religions.

@ Benin was once part of the Kingdom of Dahomey, which began in the 1600s and lasted about 300 years. The kingdom was famous for its powerful army, and women soldiers were considered the best and bravest of all. She-Dong-Hong-Beh was a commander when she was only a teenager.

* The wonderful Pendjari National Park in Benin is one of the very few places where West African lions still roam free.

Burkina Faso

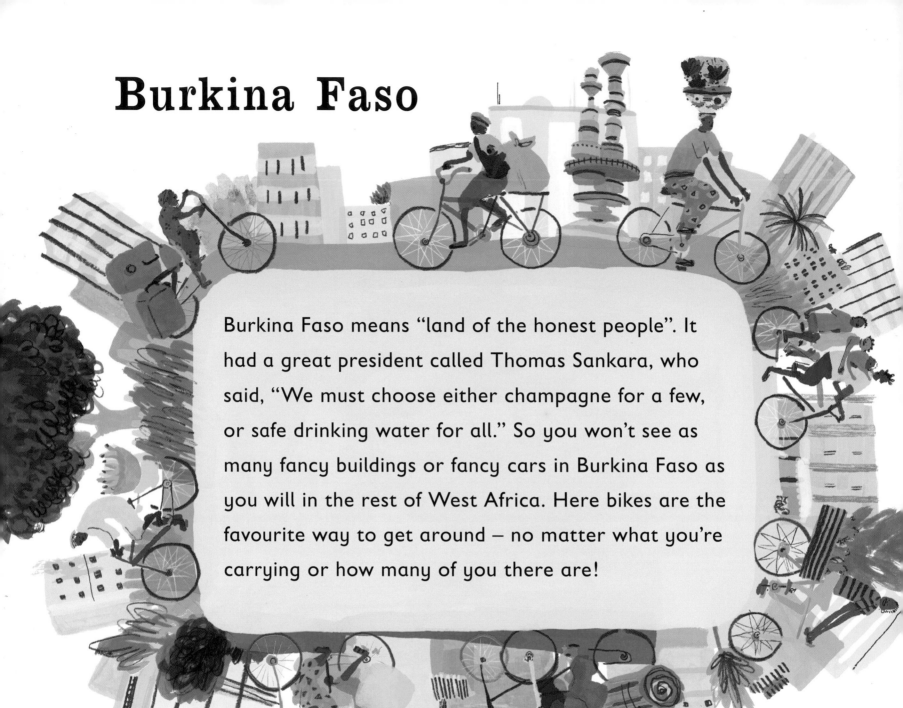

Burkina Faso means "land of the honest people". It had a great president called Thomas Sankara, who said, "We must choose either champagne for a few, or safe drinking water for all." So you won't see as many fancy buildings or fancy cars in Burkina Faso as you will in the rest of West Africa. Here bikes are the favourite way to get around – no matter what you're carrying or how many of you there are!

★ Burkina Faso has lots of big shady shea trees and sells shea butter all over the world to make creams and lotions to soften skin and hair.

◉ Caterpillars are a popular food in Burkina Faso. The yummiest are the shea caterpillars that eat only the leaves of shea trees.

Cabo Verde

Around 20 million years ago volcanoes started erupting in the Atlantic Ocean. When the volcanoes cooled down after 12 million years, the molten lava hardened into an archipelago of islands off the coast of West Africa, now called Cabo Verde. Sea levels all around the world are rising because of climate change, and one day the beautiful islands of Cabo Verde will disappear back under the sea.

★ More people from Cabo Verde live abroad in foreign countries than actually live in Cabo Verde! This is because life can be hard and scary there. Volcanoes still erupt from time to time, jobs are hard to find and sometimes all the fresh water runs out.

Côte d'Ivoire (Ivory Coast)

"Côte d'Ivoire" means "Ivory Coast". The name comes from the elephants with their huge ivory tusks that once lived there. These big beautiful elephants roamed with their families, making sure their babies always walked safely in the middle of the herd. When foreigners first arrived in Côte d'Ivoire they killed as many of the elephants as they could and sold their ivory tusks. Now more elephants are dying as their rainforest homes are destroyed and many more are still being poached. The big, loving West African forest elephants are now nearly extinct.

✱ Elephants grieve when they lose a family member, covering their bodies with leaves and visiting their graves for years and years afterwards.

★ Côte d'Ivoire is the biggest exporter of cocoa beans in the world! Maybe your favourite chocolate bar is made from cocoa that grew there.

The Gambia

This tiny country runs along the banks of the River Gambia. And there live not only Gambian people but also Gambian birds – nearly 600 different sorts. There are herons, pelicans and flamingos; guinea fowl, falcons and hoopoes; paradise fly-catchers, sunbirds and drongos. And tiny, tiny honeyguides who communicate with humans.

⊚ Gambia is the smallest country on mainland Africa. It is no more than 50 km wide in most places.

★ Gambia has more than 90 stone circles that are nearly 2,000 years old. They are believed to be built around the burial mounds of ancient kings and chiefs.

✳ Honeyguides spend their lives looking for honey. When they spot a beehive they quickly fly to a person, and whistle and whistle – calling for them to come and break open the hive. People are quick to follow because everyone loves honey!

Ghana

Ghana has the biggest market in the whole of West Africa. Thousands and thousands of people jostle their way through the walkways, buying and selling clothes and fruit, computers and cloth, dried fish and shoes, and everything else under the hot, hot sun. There are no set prices in an African market – the trader tells you what they want you to pay, and it's up to you to argue the price down. This is called haggling – it's fast and furious and full of jokes!

● "Kente" is the name of special Ghanaian cloth woven with silk and cotton. Once only members of the royal family of the Ashante kingdom were allowed to wear it. Now anyone who's rich enough to buy it can wear it.

✱ Kejetia market has around 10,000 stalls and more than 44,000 people work there. It covers 12 hectares — that is as big as a small town.

Guinea

People in Guinea love buying bright and beautiful cloth in the markets. There are so many colours and patterns to choose from. There is cloth printed like animals, cloth printed like flowers, and cloth printed with famous presidents, expensive cars, and the best mobile phones! People make it into fabulous new outfits for work and for weddings.

* The most popular cloth in Guinea is batik. Batik dyeing was invented in Indonesia. European travellers learnt it there and brought the technique with them to Africa. It is made all over the continent now.

Guinea-Bissau

Babies are tied onto their mother's backs with cloth everywhere in Guinea-Bissau. Tiny little newborn babies, small babies sucking thumbs, big babies wearing shoes – all are carried by Mama when she is cooking, or carrying water, or riding to the bank on the back of a motorbike taxi. And if Mama is resting or in the office – well, there is always a sister or a cousin to strap Baby onto.

★ Along the coast of Guinea-Bissau are mangrove swamps – tropical places where the sea turns rivers salty. Mangrove trees are the only trees in the world that can grow in salty, muddy riverbanks.

* Off the coast is a beautiful group of 88 islands called Bijagós – each one is like an island paradise where cute little pygmy hippopotamuses live!

Liberia

Liberia is Africa's oldest democratic nation and was never conquered by Europe. It was settled by African-Americans nearly 200 years ago. For centuries, African people had been kidnapped by Europeans and forced to go and work in America, Europe and the Caribbean in slavery. Years later a group returned to Africa and started their own country – Liberia, which means "Land of Freedom".

● Liberia has a special handshake. The finger-snap handshake. Look for it online!

✴ In 1995, Liberian George Weah was named African, European and World Football Player of the Year – the first footballer to ever achieve this. In 2018 he became president of Liberia.

Mali

Mali is a desert country — one of the hottest in the world. People wear billowing tunics and turbans to protect their skin from the scorching sun. Buildings are built with thick clay bricks to keep them cool and tiny windows to keep out the sun. There are whole cities made of clay in Mali — clay houses, clay mosques, clay shops and clay schools.

● Mali was the centre of one of the great African kingdoms — the Kingdom of Mali, which stretched all the way to Lake Chad in the east and to the Atlantic Ocean in the south. It was more advanced than Europe at the time and one of the largest kingdoms in the world.

★ For centuries the city of Timbuktu was an important place of learning, where Islam, medicine, surgery, science, maths, astronomy, literature and art were once studied. Its libraries still hold some of the world's most ancient manuscripts.

Niger

In Niger most people are farmers or cattle-herders. The farmers live in the wet south, where there is enough rain to grow crops. The herdsmen roam the dry north, where there is just enough grass to feed their goats and cattle and camels. Every year in the dry season, when the grass dries up, the herdsmen travel south. The farmers have harvested their crops by then and the herds can graze the stubble in the fields. Before they leave, the fields are fertilized with cattle poo – and both farmers and herdsmen are happy!

✳ Rock art in the desert in Niger shows the amazing animals that lived in the Sahara when it was a green savannah, rich in life – there are pictures of hippos and crocodiles, and life-sized carvings of giraffes. Now it is so hot that rain often evaporates before it hits the ground!

✳ Horse-racing, camel-racing and traditional wrestling and boxing are the most popular sports in Niger.

Nigeria

The city of Lagos in Nigeria is the biggest, busiest city in the whole of Africa. There are so many millions of cars that often the traffic is completely jammed for hours. So the quickest way to get around the city is on a motorbike taxi. They can weave in and out of cars, whether they are stuck or speeding. They're so dangerous they've been banned on some roads, but not everyone in Lagos obeys the rules…

◉ Nigeria has the biggest population in Africa and the biggest economy. One in four Africans is a Nigerian.

✱ The Hausa cities of Kano and Katsina in Northern Nigeria are around 1,000 years old.

★ Nigeria has the third-largest film industry after Hollywood and Bollywood – "Nollywood"!

Senegal

In Senegal, music is everywhere! It pours from open city windows, gets drummed up on village corners, and is clapped and sung in every school. Senegalese music is so infectious that it is played all over the world. American musicians who invented hip-hop and rap were heavily influenced by it. And so were jazz, blues and rock-and-roll musicians.

* The Senegalese took hundreds of their words to America – "guy" and "banana" are thought to come from Senegalese languages. Even the word "okay" may have come from the Senegalese language Wolof.

Ⓐ Sevigne Mactar Ba is a Senegalese inventor. His most famous invention is an advanced weapons rocket.

Sierra Leone

In Sierra Leone there are glass skyscrapers, marble mansions, concrete apartments and houses made of cardboard boxes and corrugated iron. There are people who own expensive cars, and people who do not even own shoes. There are families who fly abroad for holidays, and families who have to work every day of the year; even their children work – in farms and factories and collecting rubbish on the streets for recycling.

★ Sierra Leone is one of the top ten diamond-producing countries in the world – but it's not a good idea to buy diamonds from there. Diamond mining is dangerous work, often done by children forced into working by soldiers.

Togo

Food is sold on every street corner in Togo. Corn is roasted on little fires, and spicy chicken is grilled on sticks for people to buy. In roadside stores customers eat peanut stew, fried yams and prawns at rickety plastic tables. Old men sit under trees and buy the kola-nuts they love so much from girls carrying them in baskets on their heads.

● African food is popular all over the world. Africans took okra and black-eyed peas to America, and taught the European settlers there how to grow rice.

✤ People all over West Africa love to chew kola-nuts. They have more caffeine than coffee beans, and were one of the first ingredients of Coca-Cola!

Central Africa

Burundi, Cameroon, Central African Republic, Chad, Democratic Republic of the Congo, Equatorial Guinea, Gabon, Republic of the Congo and São Tomé and Príncipe.

The second biggest rainforest in the world covers Central Africa – it is loud with monkeys, parrots and trillions of insects. But it might not be there for long. Elephants and hippos evolved to make it home by becoming smaller. And so did humans. The rainforest people were the first people to live in Central Africa. They lived singing in the forest, hunting with spears and arrows. Then came those whose lifestyles now threaten the rainforest. Tall farmers from West Africa who cleared the forests for their farms, nomadic herdsmen from East Africa with cattle and goats that eat young trees, and Europeans greedy for oil, timber, mines and plantations. Some Central Africans have kept traditional lifestyles and others have chosen modern lives but, whether they are billionaires or beggars, bankers or farmers, oil-rig workers or hunters, Central Africa is home to them all!

Welcome to Central Africa!

"Balao" (Shango), "Bain veendoes!" (Portuguese), "Mbote!" (Ngala), "Boyeyi bolamu!" (Lingala) "mbote!" (Kongo)

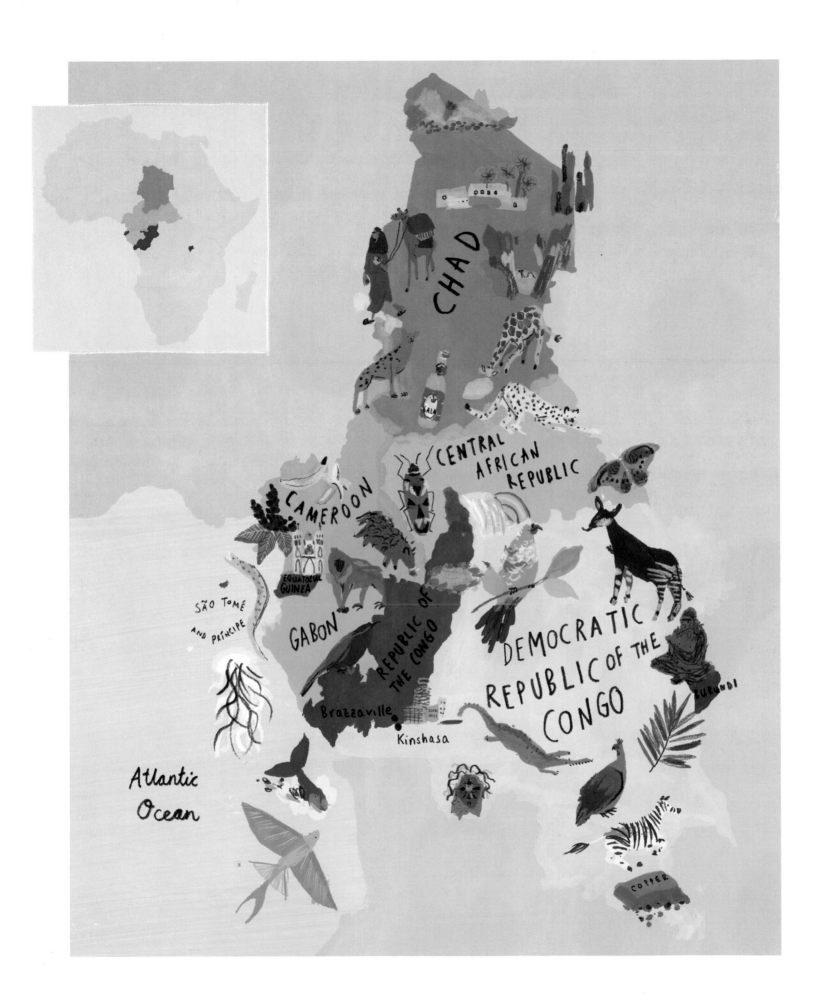

CHAD

CENTRAL AFRICAN REPUBLIC

CAMEROON

EQUATORIAL GUINEA

SÃO TOMÉ AND PRÍNCIPE

GABON

REPUBLIC OF THE CONGO

DEMOCRATIC REPUBLIC OF THE CONGO

BURUNDI

Brazzaville

Kinshasa

Atlantic Ocean

COPPER

African Hairstyles

In Africa most people's hair is very thick and very very curly. It can get into impossible tangles. For this reason lots of women wear their hair in the most amazing plaits.

On special occasions (and on bad-hair days) in lots of African countries women wear elaborate and eye-catching headscarves.

In many African countries women wear the hijab. But in others it is men who cover their heads, and sometimes their faces too.

  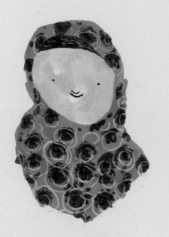  

Burundi

In Burundi, boys are taught to play huge drums by their fathers. It takes years and years of practice to be a drummer. You have to be able to dance, do acrobatics, and march balancing a huge drum on your head – while drumming like crazy at the same time! The rhythms of Burundi drumming are powerful enough to make the whole world want to dance!

● Drums in Burundi are made from a tree that grows nowhere else in the world: the "umuvugangoma" tree.

✲ The Royal Drummers of Burundi are powerful, ear-splitting and awesome. Go online and hear for yourself!

Cameroon

In Cameroon, like all over Africa, some children are driven to school by their parents, and play computer games when they get home. Other children have to walk to school no matter how far it is. Some of them wake at 4 a.m. and walk a long way to school, creeping past wild animals. Afterwards they work in the fields before doing their homework, and they don't have any devices to play on. But no matter how hard it is, children in Cameroon are determined to go to school. They all want the chance to become mechanics, doctors, lawyers, teachers and scientists.

* Cameroon grows food that kids love all over the world – bananas, peanuts, sugar and cocoa for chocolate. The people who grow them are often very poor because they are not paid enough for all their work.

Sometimes they can't even afford to eat the things they grow for us! If you buy food that is labelled "Fairtrade" then you know the farmers have been paid fairly for all their hard work.

Central African Republic

The Central African Republic is hundreds of miles from the sea on a huge high plateau covered with grassy savannah and thick forests. Through the forests millions of butterflies flutter like flowery jewels. Over the savannah the skies are lit with stars as big and bright as diamonds. And under the Central African Republic's soil lies more treasure – gold, uranium, oil and diamonds.

⊚ There are more than 600 species of butterfly in the Central African Republic.

✱ The needle in a normal, magnetic compass points north (nearly everywhere on Earth).

But don't get lost in the Central African Republic – the magnetic field under the ground is unusually strong, which makes the needles in compasses go haywire.

Chad

Most people speak two, three, four or five languages in Chad. There are over 120 languages in total so no one can speak them all! To make sure people can understand each other there are two official languages that everyone learns: Arabic and French. But people don't speak them the way they're spoken in the rest of the world – they have their own Chadian versions. Language is like nature – it evolves.

◉ Chad is named after its biggest lake – Lake Chad. One thousand years ago it was the biggest lake in the world. It is now far smaller and shrinking because of climate change. But dust from the dried-up lake still blows across the Atlantic, all the way to South America.

Democratic Republic of the Congo

There are so many rivers in the Democratic Republic of the Congo that it is easier and quicker to get around by boat than by road. Children paddle to school in canoes. Businessmen go to work in speed-boats. And everyone goes to visit family and friends using the ferries that steam up and down the Congo River for weeks and weeks and weeks. People sleep and cook and even shop on board. Just watch out for crocodiles!

⚜ There are huge mines of casserite and coltan in the Democratic Republic of the Congo. Lucky — because we can't make mobile phones and handheld devices without them.

★ There are some weird and wonderful animals in the Congo. The Okapi looks like a cross between a giraffe and a horse and has a tongue 45 cm long.

Equatorial Guinea

In Equatorial Guinea it can rain for months and months and months. Then comes the dry season when it won't rain for months and months and months. The sun gets hotter, the rivers dry up, and the ground turns to dust. When the rainy season comes back, children dance in the warm, fat, splashing raindrops. Everybody is glad that the grass and fields will turn green again … except people whose cars get stuck in the mud!

✱ Equatorial Guinea has both mainland and islands. When it is the rainy season on the mainland, the islands are usually dry. And when it is the rainy season on the islands, the mainland is usually dry.

● Equatorial Guinea makes its money from oil, which is sold all over the world to make petrol and plastic.

Gabon

In Gabon, the dark rainforest stretches right down to the beaches of the wild Atlantic Ocean. And there, both forest animals and ocean animals come out to play. Sea turtles wander in the shade of the trees and lay their eggs in the sand. Elephants splash with their babies in the shallows. And huge hippos surf the waves.

★ The government in Gabon is working hard to protect all its wonderful animals – even the oceans are a national park! Poachers only kill animals because it earns them good money. For example if people stop buying ivory then poachers will stop killing elephants.

Republic of the Congo

Lake Tele in the Congo is where the Mokele-Mbembe lives. You've not heard of the Mokele-Mbembe? It's as big as a dinosaur and as scary as a monster and it hides in the lake like a crocodile. You don't believe me? Oh well, not everybody believes in the Mokele-Mbembe. And not everybody believes in his cousin the Loch Ness monster in Scotland either!

● Some African tales are more than 60,000 years old: the fact that they have never been forgotten even though they are not written down shows what brilliant stories they are.

✱ The capital city of the Congo, Brazzaville, is just across the river from the capital of the Democratic Republic of the Congo, Kinshasa. They're talked about like two sisters in a story, one friendly and beautiful, the other dangerous and scary. But which is which?

São Tomé and Príncipe

São Tomé and Príncipe is a country made up of two islands and four islets in the Atlantic Ocean. Rainforests cover the islands' mountains, turning them emerald green. Fishermen drop their nets into crystal-clear blue water. Tourists lie on the white sandy beaches. And farmers grow cocoa — to make the chocolate and sweet things we love to eat so much.

★ São Tomé and Príncipe grows a lot of the cocoa in the world. Cocoa beans are not only used to make chocolate, they are used to make beauty creams too.

North Africa

Algeria, Egypt, Libya, Mauritania, Morocco, Tunisia and Western Sahara

North Africa is desert country, and the desert is called the Sahara. It is harder to cross than the Mediterranean Sea. This means North African customs and traditions have more in common with the Middle East and Europe than with the rest of Africa. That's because for millenia the Middle East and Europe were easier to get to! The Romans, Greeks, and Turks all conquered North Africa and made it part of their empires. And then Morocco conquered Southern Europe and made it part of their huge North African empire. Until the nineteenth century, North Africans took slaves from countries as far north as Iceland. The few North Africans who did manage to cross the Sahara before the days of planes were nomadic Berber merchants, the original North African

people, with their long lines of camels carrying salt and gold. Wherever they stopped people came to buy and sell goods. Those trading places became huge markets and those markets became the great North African cities of today. You can still buy anything there, from a computer chip to a fossil the size of a car. In fact it is said that if you cannot buy something in the markets of North Africa then you cannot buy it anywhere in the world!

Welcome to North Africa!

"AhLaN wa SahLaN!"
(Arabic)

"Amrehba Sisswene"
(Berber)

"Bienvenue!"
(French)

Football is Best

The African continent is crazy about football. It was played here long before the international rules of the game were decided in 1860.

Some people in Africa like wrestling and boxing, other people like canoeing and basketball, some are fans of cricket and rugby, but everybody is passionate, crazy, mad about football.

The weather is mostly warm enough to play outside all year round. And most children don't have expensive toys and gadgets to distract them from playing footie. Rich kids wear Adidas and Nike. Poor kids wear rags, but in the beautiful game it's only speed and skill that count.

Every two years it's the Africa Cup of Nations – the biggest tournament in Africa. So far Egypt has won it more times than any other country. People all over Africa follow the tournament but they follow other leagues too. Everyone has their favourite European clubs, where a lot of the best players are African!

Algeria

In Algeria women work everywhere – in shops, schools, offices, businesses, hospitals, courts and mosques. More than half of all university students are women. And so many doctors, scientists, lawyers and judges are women too. Cave paintings in the Algerian desert show people hunting the herds of animals that lived there thousands of years ago when the Sahara desert was lush, rich savannah. But now most people live on the coast – where the climate is just like California – because the rest of the country is either snowy mountains or scorching desert.

@ Algeria is the largest country in Africa.

✱ Soon Algeria will have one of the biggest solar energy farms in the world.

Egypt

Egypt is probably the most well-known African country. Tourists love visiting its famous pyramids and taking boat rides down the magnificent River Nile where the biggest crocodiles in Africa live. The river runs through the capital city of Cairo. It's a gigantic city with one of the best universities, and the best army, in the whole of Africa.

★ Egypt is the largest Arab country in the whole world, and is on two continents: Africa and Asia.

◉ Because most of Egypt is desert,

99% of Egyptian people live in only 3% of the country — along the edges of the River Nile. Without this wide wet river, which brings rich soil as well as water, Egypt would never have become a great nation.

Libya

The Libyan desert in the Sahara is one of the hottest and driest in the world. Sometimes ten, twenty or even thirty years go past without rain! Even the Berbers and the desert-loving Bedouins will not go into parts of the Libyan desert. They prefer their beautiful cities, built around oases. The most beautiful Berber city is Ghadames, "Pearl of the Desert". Once, only men walked its winding streets, while women visited each other in their joined-up roof gardens. Now in Libyan cities men and women walk together, and sit together in cafés, drinking coffee and laughing with their children.

* There are the ruins of a Greek temple to Zeus near the Libyan port of Cyrene. There are also the awesome ruins of an enormous Roman city called Leptis Magna. Home to the Roman emperor Septimius Severus, it was nearly as important as Rome.

* One of the oldest Jewish communities in the world was in Libya. It dated back to 300 BCE, when the ancient Greeks ruled.

Mauritania

The country of Mauritania stretches deep into the Sahara desert and down into the Sahel. "Sahel" means shoreline in Arabic – the shoreline of a desert as wide as the ocean. It is a dry and dusty land with thorny trees and prickly bushes and spiky grasses. Luckily Mauritania is full of oases too, where springs of clean water bubble up from the dry ground – and where trees, farms and whole towns can grow.

★ The desert is growing and towns and villages are being buried under sand dunes. People are escaping to the capital city on the coast which is now crowded with refugees.

* There is still slavery in Mauritania: people are bought and sold as if they are animals. They have no rights over where they live, who they live with, or what they do with each moment of their lives.

Morocco

In the heart of every North African city is a medina — the old town. In the heart of the medina is the souk — the ancient market where the camel traders who criss-crossed the Sahara sold all they'd bought. The souk in the Moroccan city of Marrakesh is so big that it covers 19 km! There are spices, carpets, leather, gold, olives and hundreds of other things for sale — just like there were a thousand years ago. And now there are watches, phones, cameras too.

● Medinas all have narrow and winding, maze-like streets. The streets are narrow to keep out the scorching desert sun. They are winding to keep out the sands of sandstorms that can bury cities alive. They are maze-like to confuse enemy raiders!

✻ Renault and PSA Peugeot Citroën have factories in Morocco, busy making cars.

Tunisia

In Tunisia, beautiful golden-domed mosques, high spiky cathedrals and cool tiled synagogues crowd together, where Muslim and Christian and Jewish people go to pray. On the shady streets outside, families sit in restaurants and cafés eating their favourite foods. Some prefer fast food while others tuck into traditional stews served with couscous and flat bread – but everyone loves to drink the super-sweet mint tea!

● Stews are cooked all over North Africa in thick pottery dishes with lids shaped like cones. The stews are made by putting pieces of meat or chickpeas in the bottom and sprinkling them with tagine spices. Vegetables are layered in a pyramid shape on the top and the dish is covered and cooked in the red hot embers of a fire.

❋ Tunisia sells more olives than almost anywhere else in the world. Lots of people have jobs looking after the olive trees and harvesting the olives. Other people work in the many, many factories in Tunisia that make clothes and shoes and car parts and electronic machinery.

Western Sahara

Western Sahara is where the Sahrawi people live. They call their country the Sahrawi Arab Democratic Republic. The Moroccan government took over Western Sahara in 1975, saying it was part of Morocco. The Sahrawi people are still fighting against this – they want to rule themselves. Once, the Sahrawi men roamed with their herds looking for grass while the women stayed at home in charge of the families, the finances and the law. Now most Sahrawi people live in refugee camps waiting for the war to end.

☆ The Sahrawi people love to drink green tea. They say the first cup is bitter, like life. The second cup is gentle, like death. And the third cup is sweet, like love.

★ The Sahara International Film festival takes place in Western Sahara every year. It is the only film festival in the world that takes place in a refugee camp.

Index

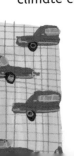

Find Out More

More facts and figures: **factmonster.com/countries**

More about African languages: **omniglot.com**

More about African music: **www.worldmusic.net/guide/**

More about African geography: **dkfindout.com/uk/earth/continents/Africa** and
nationalgeographic.org/encyclopedia/africa-physical-geography

More about African wildlife: **gowild.wwf.org.uk/Africa**
and the David Attenborough documentary *Africa* (2013, BBC)

For animated cartoons set in Africa: **binoandfino.com**

And for stories set in Africa: **www.booksfortopics.com/africa**

Atinuke is the Nigerian-born author of the bestselling Anna Hibiscus and No. 1 Car Spotter series. She started her career as an oral storyteller of tales from the African continent; now she draws on her recent Yoruba ancestry to write about contemporary life in Nigeria. Visit her website at **atinuke-author.weebly.com**

Illustrator **Mouni Feddag** was born in Nottingham to an Algerian father and an English mother. She grew up in Frankfurt, Germany, where she studied graphic design; her previous work includes illustrations for *Aquila*, Wacom and Anthropologie. This is her first book for children. Visit her website at **www.mounifeddag.com**